# AFFIRMATIONS TO PRACTICE
# HONORING YOURSELF

# Affirmations to Practice Honoring Yourself

N ESQUIRE

ISBN 979-8-218-76495-1

For you to know that you do not have to go through life's tests and trials alone. When in doubt, just *honor yourself.*

# AUTHOR'S NOTE

This collection of affirmations was birthed from my casebook, *You Have the Final Say in Matters of Your Life*. My purpose is to affirm that honoring yourself is an honorable act to do every day. When you honor yourself, you win and reap intangible rewards, even if it appears otherwise in the eyes of others. Therefore, each affirmation speaks and holds that truth.

May you pass your tests and trials and know that you're worthy of being honored.

N Esquire

# Continuing Education

*Knowledge of self is preparation for the lifelong practice of honoring yourself. You are the most important subject in your life. Honor your truth.*

## ~ 1 ~

## AFFIRMATION

I am continuing my education on self because I am worth the invest-ment.

## ~ 2 ~

## AFFIRMATION

The burden is on me to question
and seek the answers within me.

## ~ 3 ~

## AFFIRMATION

I know that infinite outcomes exist
in my life, and I choose the best
outcome.

## ~ 4 ~

## AFFIRMATION

I am exceptional and create my own rules and code of conduct to abide by.

## ~ 5 ~

## AFFIRMATION

I know that ignorance of myself is
not an excuse.

## ~ 6 ~

## AFFIRMATION

My internal rules and code of conduct trump everything outside of me.

## ~ 7 ~

## AFFIRMATION

I am prepared for "just in case" situations.

## ~ 8 ~

## AFFIRMATION

I have a master's degree in honoring myself.

# ~ 9 ~

## AFFIRMATION

I study other people's cases to miti-
gate unfavorable outcomes in my
life.

## ~ 10 ~

## AFFIRMATION

I am the primary source and my life
is a case study.

# ~ 11 ~

## AFFIRMATION

I am in control of how I perceive my matters.

## ~ 12 ~

## AFFIRMATION

What an *Honor* it is to ask myself
what do I want the desired outcome
to be.

# Honorable Acts

Practice honoring yourself now. Every
test or trial is an opportunity to act in
your best interests.

# ~ 13 ~

## AFFIRMATION

Honoring myself is a win in my casebook.

# ~ 14 ~

## AFFIRMATION

I have the final say in matters of my life.

# ~ 15 ~

## AFFIRMATION

No one is more qualified than me to
advocate on my behalf.

# ~ 16 ~

## AFFIRMATION

I practice self-advocacy every day.

# ~ 17 ~

## AFFIRMATION

I CRACk issues like an *Esquire* before they manifest into serious matters that may require legal intervention.

# ~ 18 ~

## AFFIRMATION

I learn from my losses and win the next test or trial.

## ~ 19 ~

## AFFIRMATION

I bring the facts and supporting evidence to my table for review.

## ~ 20 ~

## AFFIRMATION

I think about the matter and then
take my own advice.

## ~ 21 ~

## AFFIRMATION

I see opportunities to honor myself
instead of spotting issues.

## ~ 22 ~

## AFFIRMATION

I make a *motion* by taking action steps towards my desired outcome.

## ~ 23 ~

## AFFIRMATION

I trust my judgment and uphold my
decision.

## ~ 24 ~

### AFFIRMATION

I deserve to award myself when I
win my cases.

# ~ 25 ~

## AFFIRMATION

It is impossible to lose when I honor myself.

## ~ 26 ~

## AFFIRMATION

There is no one to appeal my final decision to but me, and I reserve the right to change my decision.

## ~ 27 ~

### AFFIRMATION

When choosing an advocate to handle my matters, I do my due diligence and assess their character and fitness to practice on my case.

## ~ 28 ~

## AFFIRMATION

I require third party advocates to have experience honoring themselves and getting favorable outcomes.

## ~ 29 ~

## AFFIRMATION

In my practice, I am mastering my analytical, reading and communication skills.

# ~ 30 ~

## AFFIRMATION

I speak my truth and know that
multiple truths exist.

# ~ 31 ~

## AFFIRMATION

A law degree or license does not determine if I am the best advocate. I am the best.

# ~ 32 ~

## AFFIRMATION

I do not have to go through life's tests and trials alone. I have guides to help me pass them.

# ~ 33 ~

## AFFIRMATION

If there is an attempt to dishonor
me, I create a case example to
honor myself.

# ~ 34 ~

## AFFIRMATION

I set the *bar* high for myself.

## ~ 35 ~

## AFFIRMATION

I act in good faith and with integrity.

# ~ 36 ~

## AFFIRMATION

I am accountable for my thoughts and actions and hold others accountable for theirs.

# ~ 37 ~

## AFFIRMATION

After I make a decision, I do not argue. I rest my case.

# ~ 38 ~

## AFFIRMATION

I am indebted to no one because I
win my cases.

# ~ 39 ~

## AFFIRMATION

When situations arise, I create free
time to consult with myself and
think about the matter.

## ~ 40 ~

## AFFIRMATION

I use external rules and resources strategically to bolster my decision and leverage success.

~ 41 ~

## AFFIRMATION

My final decision means I said what
I said, no exceptions.

# ~ 42 ~

## AFFIRMATION

I cannot afford the costs of poor advocacy or dishonoring myself.

## ~ 43 ~

## AFFIRMATION

I honor myself by managing the ex-
pectations of others of what works
or does not work best for me.

# ~ 44 ~

## AFFIRMATION

Honoring myself is my responsibility.

# ~ 45 ~

## AFFIRMATION

Asserting my right to honor myself
is not adversarial. It is honorable.

## ~ 46 ~

### AFFIRMATION

I know what I want and reject anything that is unaligned with my desired outcome.

# ~ 47 ~

## AFFIRMATION

In the case of me versus any situation, I win when I honor myself (even if external circumstances appear otherwise).

# ~ 48 ~

## AFFIRMATION

The more self-mastered I am, the better the outcomes I get in my life.

# ~ 49 ~

## AFFIRMATION

I respect other people's choices and do my best not to judge them because I do not know the facts and background of their case. Others respect and do not judge my decisions either.

# ~ 50 ~

## AFFIRMATION

I honor my truth and nothing but my truth.

# ~ 51 ~

## AFFIRMATION

Practice leads to self-mastery.

## ~ 52 ~

## AFFIRMATION

No adverse judgment can be formed
against me.

## ~ 53 ~

## AFFIRMATION

I do not fear making mistakes. Trial and error are part of self-mastery and growth.

## ~ 54 ~

## AFFIRMATION

I empower others to honor themselves.

~ 55 ~

## AFFIRMATION

I am immune from unfavorable outcomes because I committed no
wrong in honoring myself.

# FINAL JUDGMENT

*You win. Case closed.*